Egil Grislis

PROTESTANT CATHOLICITY

The Relevance of Reformation Studies
THE CADOUX LECTURE FOR 1959

The Protestant Tradition and Christian Unity
THE SCOTT LIDGETT LECTURE FOR 1959
DELIVERED BEFORE THE ANNUAL CONGRESS OF
THE FREE CHURCH FEDERAL COUNCIL

PROTESTANT CATHOLICITY

TWO LECTURES

by

GORDON RUPP

LONDON
THE EPWORTH PRESS

FIRST PUBLISHED IN 1960

© THE EPWORTH PRESS 1960

Book Steward
FRANK H. CUMBERS

SET IN MONOTYPE CASLON OLD FACE AND PRINTED IN
GREAT BRITAIN BY THE CAMELOT PRESS LTD
LONDON AND SOUTHAMPTON

CONTENTS

I

THE RELEVANCE OF REFORMATION STUDIES

ALL CHRISTIANS have to make Church history, but few are called to read it, and fewer still to write it. Yet from time to time the Church needs to turn to its students and its scholars for a check-up, a blood count of the condition of that living stream which is the holy tradition. This is true today of Reformation study. There are still plenty of older Protestants about who will nod their heads like Old Kaspar in the poem 'After Blenheim' and affirm 'It was a famous victory'. But there are younger voices which incline toward the scepticism of Little Wilhelmine: 'Tell us all about the war, and what they fought each other for?'

For there are not lacking voices which would proclaim the irrelevance of the Protestant Reformation. This year has seen the publication, after fifty years, of a new *Cambridge Modern History*.[1] In 1903 it was claimed in the preface that 'the main proportions . . . will be found to correspond with the relative importance of the several themes'. And it is interesting therefore to examine the changed proportions of the space devoted to religion. In the earlier

1 *The New Cambridge Modern History*, Vol. II, 'The Reformation'.

volume some four chapters were devoted to Luther and the German Reformation; now, instead of 136 pages there are 48—about a third. In 1903 Calvin had a chapter all to himself; now, instead of 35 pages, he has 7, or one-fifth. The changed perspective is perhaps indicated by the fact that there are now 20 pages devoted to 'The Economic Importance of Antwerp' and it is to be observed that the title of the next volume in the series is *The Counter Reformation and the Price Revolution*. Yet even this did not please those who hold the economic interpretation of history, and Mr Christopher Hill and Mr E. J. Hobsbawm complained in reviews that the religious chapters were dealt with by theologians. Mr A. L. Rowse complained for a different reason that there was still too much 'theological nonsense'. The shift of interest is evident. Yet one would have thought that whatever the twentieth century thinks about the irrelevance of the Christian religion, the men of the sixteenth century could not be made intelligible without it, and that any picture of the Reformation would be gross caricature which brushed aside the things which the men of that age cared about most desperately, for which they were in fact ready to break a Church, to defy a world, and to embrace cruel torture and savage death. Behind the complaints of Oxford historians against the *Cambridge History* I seem to detect a failure of nerve. The great nineteenth-century historians Froude, Carlyle, Macaulay, sat loosely to Christian orthodoxy and had a doughty anti-clericalism, but they had sense to see that religion mattered and they took pains to understand theological issues.

Behind this contemptuous dismissal of Protestant and Puritan theology there is, one suspects, real ignorance, and a funking of the chore involved in mastering the intricate code form of an alien ideology. There is no Protestant mental fashion in contemporary intellectual circles. 'It is commonly regarded as a sign of education to show an interest in Catholicism,' says Walther von Loewenich of Germany. In England, too, a century of Catholic revival, Anglican and Roman, often splendidly illuminating the field of letters, has had marked effect. Neo-Catholicism, like Neo-Thomism, may not be true but it is interesting and to be treated seriously. Even the little group of modern historians who have begun to hit out against a 'papist' view of history in which the generalizations and romanticism had far outstripped the facts, are not any nearer to a reappraisal of the Protestant tradition. We are all the lapsed heirs of the Victorian Protestants. It is understandable, if regrettable, that modern liberal historians, who know nothing of Biblical Theology and have hardly heard of the Ecumenical Movement should mistake the new Protestantism—i.e. a Protestantism ready to re-examine and reinterpret its perspectives—for a mere hangover from a now discredited sectarian interpretation of history.

There is, of course, much more than prejudice and mental fashion involved at this point: a whole balance of political, economic and religious facts involved in the interpretation of the past. But as regards the sixteenth century, we have already hinted there is prevalent a persistent playing down of religion at the expense of politics. Thus, Dr Elton's generalization, 'the mainspring of the Reformation was political',[2] (in England) seems to lead him, in the face of growing evidence, to dismiss the survival of Lollardy, and when he calls the Cambridge Reformers 'small time heretics'[3] we remember that one of them was Hugh Latimer, the greatest preacher of the age, and we wonder what the English Reformation would have been like without these men and their friends, that is, without Tyndale's Bible and Cranmer's Liturgy. Dr Hans Baron says of the Continental Reformation: 'The first place in this period was occupied by religious ideas. But they had a realistic rival . . . whether religious ideas profoundly transformed the external world in which they existed, or whether they themselves were transformed by political needs and ideals depended always on the historical environment.'[4]

Sociologists and economic historians are even more sweeping and surprisingly doctrinaire in their exaltation of the conditioning effect of material pressures. According to their view of history it

[2] *The New Cambridge Modern History*, II.228.
[3] *England under the Tudors*, p. 111.
[4] *English Historical Review*, Vol. LII (1937), p. 633.

consists of the continuous brain-washing of the theologians by the forces of history itself: what survives, after a generation, of the dynamic ideas of the intellectuals, is something which would have been strange, even repugnant to the prophetic pioneers: and what that something is, and how it has come to prevail is something to be found among what are known as non-theological factors. Thus Dr Norman Birnbaum, who is more anxious than some to allow the thinkers to have their due role can conclude: 'Religion is an interpretation of a given social situation . . . the organization of social groups and psychological processes taking place within them must affect religious innovation by setting limits to the possible interpretation of the situation.'[5]

Let it be admitted that Church historians have too long undervalued the importance of the material environment. They ought not, as believers in a religion of Incarnation, to be afraid of taking the mass of history seriously. Yet we may admit that bad history, like bad science, is, when perpetrated by Christians, only too inclined to bring in the Holy Spirit to fill in the gap. But the doctrinaire sociologist goes to the other extreme. Thus Dr Birnbaum has written a brilliant and suggestive analysis of the part played by the different social strata in the Reformation in Zürich. But his study is vitiated by a determination to make all the facts fit the pattern.

---

[5] *Social Structure and the German Reformation* (Harvard Diss., 1957), p. 455.

Thus he notes that among the opposition to Zwingli from the guilds, a high proportion came from the 'Kambel' Guild, which comprised retailers, second-hand dealers, and vendors of oil. He explains this on the theory that 'these rather traditionalized elements were unenthusiastic about the activities of the Zwinglian *élite*'.[6] But what evidence is that that second-hand dealers or oil vendors were more naturally conservative than the ancient crafts of the goldsmiths, glaziers, and artists? Yet those were, in many cities besides Zürich, allies of a Reformation which was most damaging, in this normative period, to the vested interests of their profession. On the whole we may doubt whether the 'Kambels are coming!' is an authentic war cry of the Counter Reformation in Zürich. Again, in a useful monograph published by the Karl Marx University of Leipzig, Gerhard Zschäbitz asserts that 'one reason for the swift rise of the Anabaptist movement at the turn of the third and fourth decades of the sixteenth century was the rise in prices'.[7] I simply do not believe it, and I think only ideological bigotry could support the view.

From another view, the Reformation is belittled in the interests of the History of Science. Professor Herbert Butterfield writes: 'The scientific revolution outshines everything since the rise of Christianity, and reduces the renaissance and the reformation

[6] *The Zwinglian Reformation in Zürich: Past and Present* (1959).
[7] *Zur Mitteldeutschen Wiedertäuferbewegung nach dem Grossen Bauernkrieg*, p. 160.

to the rank of mere episodes, mere internal displacements within the system of medieval Christendom.' Reformation studies, it seems, must be relegated to a sub-department of medieval history. The proper study of mankind is 'sputniks'. We need not play down the importance of the scientific revolution, and its effect on human perspective, though its ideology would never have emerged from a scientific vacuum, had it not been accompanied by a similar crisis of European conscience in the fields of politics, letters and philosophy. But we may ask, if the Christian religion be true, whether its own internal dialogue may not still be of tremendous meaning, whether in fact, a prophetic and religious movement within the Church might not discern truths about the origin and destiny of man, and of his place in the scheme of things, more important than anything which man can find with his own splendid tools? The truth is that Protestantism more than Catholicism has been closer to the spirit of each changing age, and that many of its deepest insights grow to Dominion status, so to speak, and finally go off on their own to mingle with the ideas of the world at large. And this is the truth as well as the error in those nineteenth-century Papal Encyclicals which lumped together Protestantism and unbelief, and modern thought.

The dismissal of the Reformation as part of a medieval world view is not new. It was massively affirmed thirty years ago by Ernst Troeltsch who thought the Reformers were too much involved in a medieval world to have anything genuinely new to say and who reserved his prizes for the Reformation sects, and saw the real break-through into modernity as taking place not in the sixteenth but in the eighteenth century.

All I want to do here is affirm two modest propositions. The first is that Reformation studies are an important field of historical and theological research in their own right, that they are alive and moving and opening the way to new assessments. The other is that the Reformation has a bearing on our own contemporary situation, and not least in regard to the recovery of Christian unity.

THE REVIVAL OF REFORMATION STUDIES IN THE TWENTIETH CENTURY

Calvin and Calvinism

We must begin, I think, with the revival of Calvinism associated with the work of Karl Barth. I remember walking outside Heidelberg with Martin Dibelius in 1937, and being told by him how greatly he was impressed by Barth. 'But', he said, 'I am afraid he is becoming far too much an orthodox Calvinist. It is too much "Calvin says . . .".' Well, in the last few years Barth has shaken a good many points of Calvinist orthodoxy, and yet his great *Kirchliche Dogmatik* is a great system of Protestant scholasticism, with its massive root in quotation from Scripture, the Fathers, and from the Protestant divines of the seventeenth and eighteenth centuries. It can indeed stand comparison with the great medieval *summae*, and is like theirs a noble and impressive cathedral of the mind.

For thirty years this great mind has wrestled not with marginal problems, but with the mighty themes of the Christian dimension, with the Holy Trinity, with sin and grace, with creation and redemption, with the Church. Nor has this been divorced from contemporary existence. The great Declaration of Barmen could not have been written apart from Barth's influence on the Confessing Church, for which he provided the theological nerve enabling it to face the peril of the pagan creed of National Socialism, and the heresy of the German Christians. Following the Barthian revival there has been a less spectacular revival of technical studies in Calvin, including the work of Peter Barth, and a notable series of works and translations from Dr Torrance and the Scottish theologians.[8]

Luther-studies

In the field of Luther-studies there has been an immense concentration of research in six languages and over many lands.[9] The great folio edition of Luther's Works, the *Weimarana*, which began in

[8] For an admirable summary of the latest scholarship on Calvin, see the Historical Association pamphlet, *John Calvin*, by the Rev. Basil Hall.

[9] Up-to-date Luther Bibliographies are issued each year in the *Luther Jahrbuch*, ed. Dr Franz Lau. See also the Volume *Lutherforschung heute* (Berlin, 1958).

1883, is now in sight of completion in 100 volumes—
and how that would have appalled Luther himself
who thought that only two or perhaps three of his
writings, including his little Children's Catechism,
would survive him. Very little of all this has hitherto
been available in English, but now an edition in
fifty-five volumes has been launched from Phila-
delphia and Chicago, so that Luther will soon speak
English (according to the *Chicago Manual of English
Style*) as Chaucer so nearly said of his Prioress :

> *Entunèd in the nose ful seemely*
> *After the scole of 'Philly Chicago'.*

I would not be understood to speak slightingly of the
best American Reformation scholarship, which is
indeed in this field far ahead of England. There
is a notable group of younger American scholars,
Pellikan, Quanbeck, Fischer, who are thoroughly
and technically equipped for the kind of systematic
and technical researches which are already bearing
fruit. One can only admire the way in which Roland
Bainton and William Pauck have produced a con-
stellation of fine pupils whom they have directed
toward the period of the Reformation.

Much modern research has centred on the Young
Luther. A major achievement has been the editing
and publishing of the lectures delivered by Luther
as a young Professor of Biblical Theology in Wittenberg. In these fascinating documents we can trace the
growth of the Reformer's mind ; unmelted blocks of

ice of scholasticism (Nominalism!) still float on the surface, but there are deeper currents and many intuitions profound and beautiful. A turning-point in Luther's life was when he came to a new understanding of the meaning of the phrase, 'The Righteousness of God' (*Justitia Dei*), and though we ought not to read into the affair a catastrophic conversion experience which can be pinpointed like John Wesley's 24th May at a quarter before nine, scholars have tried to find the place where the new illumination appears in his lectures. There has been a growing consensus that it was before his lectures on Romans in 1515, and I still find the evidence for this impressive. But recently there has been a turning away from these early documents, and an inclination to work back from Luther's maturity. Important essays by Wilhelm Link and Ernst Bizer[10] mark this tendency, and Professor Bizer thinks that Luther did not reach his new understanding about Justification by Faith until 1519, well after the outbreak of the Church struggle. The change of interest is likely to be fruitful, as long as we remember the danger of reading back into the young Luther the vested interests of a later Protestant orthodoxy.

For me, the exciting period is that of the Reformation before the outbreak of Protestantism, before 1527, when all is white hot, in ferment, and before it has cooled off, crystallized out, sometimes petrified

---

[10] Wilhelm Link, *Das Ringen Luthers um die Freiheit der Theologie von der Philosophie* (1955); Ernst Bizer, *Fides ex auditu* (1958).

into systems of Protestant orthodoxy. Nowadays I suppose a thesis a month appears on Luther from Scandinavia and Germany : it is too much, and there is an appalling amount of repetition, so that for the most part time is better spent reading Luther. Yet the last years have produced some important monographs. Bengt Hägglund has examined Luther's relation to Occamism, B. Lohse Luther's relation of Faith and Reason, with results which will surprise those who think of him as an irrationalist. Attention has been drawn to his use of the Bible, showing that he moves against the whole biblical material and not just the Pauline element. Dr James Atkinson of Hull is among those who have shown the importance for Luther of the Johannine theology. Walther von Loewenich has examined his use of the Synoptics, and Heinrich Bornkamm has given us a luminous study of Luther and the Old Testament, and more recently Ostergaard-Nielsen has examined Luther's doctrine of the Scripture in relation to the Living Word.[11]

Gerhard Ebeling's examination of Luther's principles of exegesis is one of the great seminal studies of the century.

The Church struggle with the Nazis raised the question, 'What was Luther's real teaching about the State?' and a small literature has sprung up since

[11] B. Hägglund, *Theologie und Philosophie bei Luther* (1955); B. Lohse, *Ratio und Fides* (1958); W. von Loewenich, *Luther als Ausleger der Synoptiker* (1954); H. Bornkamm, *Luther und das Alte Testament* (1948); Ostergaard-Nielsen, *Scriptura sacra et viva vox* (1957).

the war about Luther's teaching of the Two King-
doms. Gustav Törnvall has discussed it from the
functional point of view (what Luther calls 'Regi-
ment') of God's single Rule over His creation in
which He uses the two instruments, spiritual and
earthly government. Franz Lau and Paul Althaus
have stressed Luther's other institutional word
'*Reich*', and have examined the responsibilities of
Christians who have a double citizenship. Johannes
Heckel in an important study, *Lex Charitatis*, raised
the question of the possibility of Church law on
Luther's principles. There has been alongside this a
lively discussion of Luther's doctrine of the Church,
and two recent essays may be mentioned, one by
Ernst Kinder who finds interesting agreements as
well as disagreements between Luther and Augustine, and the other from one who writes far too little
but always profoundly, Joachim Iwand of Bonn.[12]

Ulrich Zwingli

But what do they know of Luther, who only Luther
know? There has been an awakening of research into
the other patterns of Reformation, in the great cities
of Augsburg, Nuremberg, Strasbourg, and above all in

---

[12] G. Ebeling, *Luthers Hermeneutik* (1941); G. Törnvall, *Ändligt och världsligt
regemente hos Luther* (1940) (see also G. Wingren, *Luthers lära om Kallelsen*;
F. Lau, *Luthers Lehre von den beiden Reichen* (1953). J. Heckel, *Lex Charitatis*
(1953). This has given rise to a small literature of its own. See especially J.
Heckel, *Im Irrgarten der Zwei-Reiche-Lehre* (Munich, 1957), and F. E. Cranz,
Luther on Justice, Law, Society (Harvard, 1959); E. Kinder, in *Festschrift fur
J. Lortz* (1958); J. Iwand, in *Festschrift fur G. Dehn* (1958).

the Swiss centres of Zürich, Basel, Berne and Geneva.

The old picture of Zwingli as the intellectual, the political parson, has to be greatly modified. It was always belied by the Zürich Bible which he edited, and by the invitation which he put on the cover of his books, and at the heart of his liturgy: 'Come unto me, all ye that labour and are heavy-laden.' Some Swiss scholars have gone to the other extreme. Nowadays it seems that in order to attract ecumenical attention a theologian must be shown to be (*a*) Theocentric, (*b*) Eschatological, (*c*) Existential. Recent writings by Rich and Locher perhaps press too hard in these directions. But Oscar Farner's fine but sadly unfinished biography in three volumes is an admirable corrective to theological '*Tendenz*'. Walther Köhler has produced a useful study of Zwingli, and in his great two-volume work *Zwingli und Luther* he has given us the book to end all books on the eucharistic controversy of the 1520s and 1530s. There are two fine, amply-documented articles on Zwingli and Zwinglianism in the French *Dictionary of Catholic Theology*, and among monographs may be mentioned a study of Zwingli's liturgical writings by a Lutheran, Schmidt-Clausing, and an examination by Roger Ley of his attitude toward Church discipline.[13]

[13] A. Rich, *Die Anfänge der Theologie H. Zwinglis* (1949); G. W. Locher, *Die Theologie H. Zwingli im Lichte seiner Christologie*, Vol. I (1952); O. Farner, *H. Zwingli*, 3 Vols; W. Köhler, *H. Zwingli* (1952); *Zwingli und Luther*, 2 Vols (1953); Schmidt-Clausing, *Zwingli als Liturgiker*; R. Ley, *Kirchenzucht bei Zwingli* (1948); H. Schmidt, *Zwinglis Lehre von der göttlichen und menschlichen Gerechtigkeit* (Zürich, 1959).

Dr Bromiley has compiled a useful volume on Zwingli and Bullinger in the *Library of Christian Classics* (XXIV). It includes that extraordinary description of heaven which he addressed to the King of France: 'There you will see Adam, Enoch, Noah, Abraham, David . . . Peter, Paul: Hercules too and Phineas, Socrates, Aristides . . . Louis the Pious, and all your predecessors the Louis, the Phillips, Pepins and all your ancestors.' This benevolent eclecticism, worthy of a modern University school of Comparative Religion, has been examined by Rudolf Pfister in a significant study, *The Blessedness of the Elect Heathen in Zwingli* (1952). There have been interesting studies of Bullinger, who succeeded Zwingli after the fatal battle of Cappel in 1531 and who conducted a vast correspondence of which some 12,000 letters have survived, and there have been books by Bouvier and Walser, and an interesting study by Helmuth Kressner on the influence of Bullinger's Zürich on the Elizabethan reformation in England.[14]

Martin Bucer

In the year 1523 there came to the city of Strasbourg a former Dominican monk alone, unemployed, unknown; yet within a few months this man, Martin Bucer, had become the soul of the Reformation in that great Imperial city. About Bucer a mass of new

14 Walser, *Die Predestination bei Bullinger* (1958); H. Kressner, *Schweizer Ursprünge des anglikanischen Staatskirchentums* (1953).

material is forthcoming. When I was in Strasbourg in 1937 there was a whole cupboard full of unpublished MSS in the Thomas-Stift, and now there is to be the first edition of Bucer's writings in French and German under the editorship of Drs Wendel and Stupperich. How fruitful this will be can be judged from a kind of preview, a fascinating volume by the Dominican, J. V. Pollet, *Martin Bucer: Studies in his Correspondence,* which contains hitherto unknown documents which shed light not only on the Strasbourg Reformation, but on the Reformation in Germany and England.[15] At the end of his life Bucer went into exile, to that distant backward land called England, and became Professor of Divinity in Cambridge. There he shivered in the dank mists of our English fens until Edward VI gave him a stove, behind which he sat warm, sniffing nostalgic blasts of continental brimstone. In return he wrote the great book, *De Regno Christi,* summing up the experience of a life-time of practical reform, and giving a noble premonition of Puritan England. It has now been admirably edited in Latin and French by Professor Wendel, and is the firstfruits of the new Buceran corpus.[16]

His liturgical experiments were of outstanding importance, though they suffered from his incurable verbosity, which, with his almost unintelligible handwriting must have made him rather a trial to his

---

[15] *Martin Bucer: Etudes de la Correspondance* (1959).
[16] *Martini Buceri: Opera Latina,* Vols XV and XV *bis.*, ed. F. Wendel.

colleagues. There is a useful study here in rather weird English by a Dutchman, Van der Poll: *Martin Bucer's Liturgical Ideas* (1954). About his theology there have been useful studies by Eells, Strohl, Heinrich Bornkamm, and August Lang.[17] Lang calls Bucer 'the Pietist among the Reformers' and a good case might be made for him as the first Methodist, for he laid great stress on hymn-singing, Christian experience, and personal holiness. But Lang rather over-stresses Bucer's Reformed Church-manship and in this has been followed by Dr Torrance. On Bucer in England Constantine Hopf has written a difficult book which is a collection of learned footnotes. Some older writers exaggerated the influence of Bucer and the other foreign refugee scholars, Peter Martyr and John a Lasco, on the English Prayer Books and on Archbishop Cranmer's theology of the eucharist. Recently Dr Dugmore has been concerned to show that Cranmer and Ridley had minds of their own and had read the 'old Fathers' on their own account.[18] But perhaps he does not do justice to the immense experience of these exiles in this matter.

Imagine the captain of a village cricket team who discovered on the eve of the great match with Little Snodgrass that Lock and Laker and Trueman

---

[17] H. Strohl, *La Pensée de la Reforme* (1951), and *Bucer, humaniste Chrétien* (1939). H. Bornkamm, *Martin Bucers Bedeutung* (1952; with an important Bucer bibliography by Stupperich). A. Lang, *Puritanismus und Pietismus* (1941).
[18] C. Dugmore, *The Mass and the Reformers* (1959).

were staying in the village. Would he not seek their advice about 'how to get the beggars out'? Would he not, if he could, smuggle them into his team disguised as the baker's second cousin and the undertaker's nephew and the new assistant curate? And remember, Martin Bucer was the greatest ecclesiastical spin bowler of the age, the very model of a modern ecumenical.

The Anabaptists and Radicals

But the really exciting new field concerns the radical Reformers. Puritanism as well as Protestantism began in Wittenberg, with Andrew Carlstadt as prototype of that perennial Protestant figure who is always with us, the 'awkward squad'. His writings have been little known (there are some 35 of his pamphlets in the John Rylands Library, Manchester) and it is useful that some of them are now being published, by Kaehler and by Herztsch, for they had much influence alongside the little mystical tract *Theologia Germanica* on the radicals in the years 1523-4.[19] The Russians have discovered a reformation of their own, what they call the real 'People's Reformation', and of it the hero is no longer Luther, the bourgeois reactionary, but Thomas Müntzer, that strange genius who was the fanatical leader of the Peasant War in Saxony. The best study of him from behind the Iron Curtain is a massive book by

---

[19] Kaehler, *Karlstadt und Augustin* (1952); E. Herztsch, *Karlstadts Schriften*, I and II (1957).

M. M. Smirin which was awarded the Stalin Prize (Second Class).[20]

Müntzer's writings were edited by Brandt, his letters by Kirn and Böhmer ; and useful monographs have been written by Seidemann, Lohmann, and Hinrichs. There have been interesting discussions by Oskar Mehl of Müntzer's extremely original liturgical and musical experiments.

The Anabaptists have been the Cinderella of Reformation History.[21] Persecuted by Protestant and Catholic alike, denigrated and caricatured by orthodoxy, discredited by their own extremists, they are now being startlingly rehabilitated. An immense amount of new information is being published in volumes of sources in Germany and in Switzerland. In the interpretation of the evidence we owe much to the American Mennonite historians, led by Dr Bender, who have made their *Mennonite Quarterly* an almost indispensable tool in this field and whose four-volume *Mennonite Encyclopaedia* contains scores of articles with material not elsewhere available in English. Dr Bender has stressed the importance of the Swiss Brethren of Zürich and has given us a life of Conrad Grebel, the leader of the group of 'angry young men' who broke away from the leadership of Zwingli in 1523. Professor Fritz Blanke of Zürich has written usefully about these men.

[20] M. M. Smirin, *Thomas Müntzer und der grosse Bauernkrieg* (1956); A. Meusel, *Thomas Müntzer und seine Zeit* (1952).

[21] A very full Anabaptist bibliography is to be found in the American review, *Church History*, by G. H. Williams (March and September 1958).

The tendency of the American writers is to make these Anabaptists far too tidy, too quiet and respectable, for if they had as Dr Payne has pointed out, a higher proportion of martyrs than any other Reformation movement, they had also a higher proportion of really 'wild men'. A recent volume of essays, *The Rediscovery of the Anabaptist Vision*, suffers from this defect. The same must be said of Dr F. H. Littell's *The Anabaptist View of the Church* (2nd edn, 1959). But this is an important work, a mixture of profundity and naïvety but with deep erudition in the German sources. Dr Littell shows us the core of the Anabaptist theology where we might not have expected it, in their doctrine of the Church. He illustrates their conception of their own vocation as a covenanted people, a 'Church under the Cross'; their conception of a Fall of Christianity in the early centuries, and its restitution in this, the last age; and above all a sense of missionary vocation for which we look in vain to the great Reformers (with the one exception of Bucer) and which took urgently and practically the missionary commission in Matthew 28 and Mark 16.

Attention has recently turned from the Swiss Brethren to the South German Anabaptists. Fellmann has given us a fine edition of the writings of the Nuremberg schoolmaster, Hans Denck. Notable among these was a disciple of Müntzer, Hans Huth, a wandering prophet, a kind of Anabaptist Pied Piper. One day last summer I sat in the Cathedral of

Augsburg, with its vivid memories of the Reforma-
ion, where the great reformers and humanists
preached against the Anabaptists. It was oddly
moving to go from there and to ponder in the
Staatsarchiv near by a bundle of faded documents,
some of them in the great humanist scholar Peutinger's
handwriting, of the examinations of Hans Huth in
1528, beginning with so-called 'friendly interroga-
tion' and going on to examination under torture,
first the weights and then the rack, and to the final
note: 'The prisoner Hans Huth died yesterday
afternoon at 3 o'clock, from burns received while
trying to escape.' It was a grim reminder of the war
crimes of the Protestant civil war which began in
1525, amid which these haunted, hunted men
presented a shocking, challenging emblem of the
simplicity of the apostolic Church. In the last
month studies of other Anabaptist figures have
appeared, of Melchior Hoffman, Felix Manz, Lud-
wig Hetzer (a most able study this by Dr Goeters),
and Pilgram Marbeck.

Marbeck is another notable person. He was an
engineer of genius. He devised a scheme for
floating logs from the Black Forest over a series of
canals into the city of Strasbourg. Though he made
no secret of his Anabaptist profession, neither here
nor in Augsburg later could the authorities afford to
lose his services and almost alone of the leaders he
died in his bed. He was a lay theologian of no mean
order and of a remarkably unsectarian temper, in

short a very civil engineer. In 1956 a volume of MSS called the *Kunstbuch*, some four hundred pages of mostly unknown tracts and letters by Marbeck and his friends, was discovered in the Bürgerbibliothek in Berne. Here is exciting new material. Finally three works in English must be mentioned: the very useful volume of sources edited by Professor G. H. Williams, Vol. XXV in the *Library of Christian Classics* (*Anabaptist and Spiritual Writers*, 1957), an admirable survey of the whole movement by Dr Ernest Payne in the new volume of the *Cambridge Modern History*, and a balanced and scholarly account of Anabaptist origins by Dr Morris West in a symposium *Baptism*, edited by A. Gilmore (1959).

Dr Littell is surely right when he says that this new material demands a reassessment of the Anabaptists, and also of what he calls the State Church theologians—which does not mean that the great Reformers were all wrong. Zwingli's noble vision of a Christian commonwealth, and of Zürich as a prophetic community, enshrined Christian verities not comprehended in the Anabaptist Vision, even as recaptured for us by American historians.

I hope I have shown that Reformation studies are alive. They are worth taking pains about, they will reward those who will trouble to acquire the technical tools. Far too many students are lazy and frightened about languages : for the sake of the spare time they will devote in two or three years to football, to television, or to murder stories, they could learn to

use German and Latin to get at the primary sources
where all the excitement lies, could buy a mental key
opening the way to refreshment which would in-
vigorate all their ministry ; for it is a great, a whole-
some thing for a busy parson in the active work to
have some such worth-while hobby of the mind to
which he can turn when harassed by the contradic-
tions of the saints.

And now we come to the great question of that
horrid child :

> *And what good came of it at last,*
> *Quoth little Peterkin?*

Shall we say that the Reformation is important
because its teachings were (*a*) Theocentric, (*b*)
Eschatological, (*c*) Existential? Shall we turn to
those great nineteenth-century slogans, what we
might call the Principles of the Reformation : The
Right of Private Judgement and the Priesthood of
All Believers? Shall we turn to the watchwords of
the Reformers themselves : '*Sola Fide: sola Gratia*',
'*Sola Scriptura*', '*Soli Deo Gloria*' ?

Is it not a more excellent way to begin with men
rather than with abstractions, with events rather than
ideas? Here is a man, a man with a bruised conscience. He seeks peace. But he finds none in the
Church and in her sacramental ministries. And this
is very strange, for the Church came into existence
for this very thing, to proclaim to sinful men the
forgiveness of their sins. And stranger still, at this

very point, where the Church should be most sensitive, there she is most obtuse, most insensitive, for here the abuses (theoretical and practical) coalesce—penance and purgatory, indulgences and invocation of saints, and private masses. This man finds consolation in the Scriptures and in prayer. He turns to tell the Church of what he has found, of this dangerous situation of which he has become aware. He speaks, but instead of finding sympathy and understanding he finds misunderstanding and suspicion, closed minds and hardened hearts, so that he begins at last to question those things which until now he has never doubted, the doctrines of the Church and of her authority. That is the story of Martin Luther.

Two years ago, at a historian's congress in Rome, I went with others into the audience chamber at the Vatican, and there over the throne were written the words from the 8th chapter of Romans: 'Whom therefore he called, them he also justified.' I do not think it would have occurred to any medieval Pope to put such a text in that place. Luther altered the theological agenda, not only of Protestantism but of the Roman Church. It is often pointed out that there are no medieval treatises on the doctrine of the Church, 'in the medieval cursus'. But there are treatises by John Wyclif and John Huss, and if the great Reformers turned to this doctrine it was because they were pressed against the fundamental question of the nature of the Church and her authority, the relative importance of Scripture and tradition. In these two great matters, the doctrine of grace and salvation, the doctrine of the Church and tradition, the Reformers proclaimed truths which we must hold in fee against the day when we begin a real dialogue with our separated brethren of the Church of Rome. And when we have admitted the blind spots, the intolerances of the Reformers themselves, it is true that at the Reformation the Church of Christ knew, under God, a new birth of freedom, which must involve entirely new considerations, a new conception of unity as we seek to mend again, in the vision of a 'Coming Great Church', that which was broken in the sixteenth century.

The Protestant Reformation is an important episode in Church History, the greatest crisis so far, it may be, in the history of the Western Church. But it will one day inevitably become remote, and the Church of God will need to turn away to other tasks. I am not at all ashamed of the word 'Protestant', but I admit that the enduring word is 'catholic' (with a small 'c'). Already the younger Churches in India, Africa and China are impatient at our preoccupation with what was after all an affair within European history. Many of the creative works of the Protestant Reformation are reaching their end as effective evangelical vehicles—the English Bible, the Prayer Book—and we shall need new creative works written from newer and more ecumenical perspectives. The great Reformers will take their place for us among the doctors of the Church but we shall think of them as Luther thought of the 'old Fathers' when he said : 'Augustine said : "Don't believe any teacher, however greatly learned, and however holy, save in so far as he teaches from holy scripture." ' 'That', said Luther, 'is how I want my books to be read.' For the meaning of Reformation studies is that the Church is not *Ecclesia Reformata*, as reformed once for all and needing never to be purged again, but *Ecclesia Reformanda*, always in reformation, always under the present, living, active role of Christ Himself, speaking by His Word, guiding by His Spirit, as it was in the beginning, is now, and ever shall be, world without end.

II

THE PROTESTANT TRADITION AND CHRISTIAN UNITY

I THINK I HAVE one qualification for delivering a
Scott Lidgett Memorial Lecture in that I am
one of John Scott Lidgett's 'sons in the Gospel',
for I began my ministry as a Methodist preacher
in that South London District of which he was the
Chairman, and received from him those kindnesses
and encouragements which mean so much to a
younger man. Moreover, I stand consciously and
gratefully in his tradition of Churchmanship—
Protestant, Free Church, Methodist with its roots
in the Evangelical Arminianism of John and Charles
Wesley. This seemed to dictate my choice of theme,
for no cause was dearer to Dr Lidgett than Christian
Unity, which he declared to be 'the primary object
which faith sets before an enlightened Christian
statesmanship'. And how better approach that
subject than from the consideration of what
for him was the great over-arching concept—
'Catholicity'?

'As we look out upon history and the world', he
wrote, 'it is with the same vision of all things in
Christ which dominates the perceptions of all
believers, without distinction of age, or race, or

Church. Not a saint, a thinker, a hero, or a martyr of the Church, but we claim a share in his character, influence and achievements, by confessing the debt we owe to the great tradition which he has enriched by saintly consecration, true thought, or noble conduct.'[1] It is the Catholicity of the hymn-book, which expresses in a sense not perhaps intended by Vincent of Lerins, what has been believed by all Christians, everywhere and at all times. Lidgett once offered to arrange a service of worship and praise in which Roman Catholics, Anglicans and all sections of Evangelical Nonconformity should take part, in which 'the hymns should celebrate the faith and experience of Christ which has been common to, say, St Bernard, Luther, Watts, the Wesleys and more besides . . . what was deepest and therefore most Catholic in the faith, experience and loyalty of them all'.[2]

He called this 'inward Catholicity'. 'There are', he said, 'two faulty because superficial ways of interpreting the catholicity of the Church. . . . The first understands by it the system of dogmatic truths which its ministry affirms, teaches and imposes . . . the second regards the church as the sphere within which . . . authority is exercised for the dispensing of ordered and external means of grace, and for the guidance and control of human conduct.' But there is a deeper catholicity. 'It consists in the fellowship of a great experience . . . fellowship with

---

[1] *The Catholicity of Methodism* (1908).   [2] *My Guided Life*, p. 250.

the saints through common access to God.'[3] Not that Lidgett undervalued dogma. He had a special devotion to the Nicene Creed. His whole career shows how much he cared for churchmanship, and for the practical expression of Christian faith in private and public life.

Now this, which he called 'inward Catholicity', was an authentic part of his inheritance. We can trace it back through Alexander Knox to John Wesley. It is a natural stress for Methodists, who began not as an institution but as a society. In an article which he wrote in 1949 Lidgett stressed this priority of the Church as society over the Church as institution, when he wrote of Methodism that 'the society, all important for the furtherance and fellowship of Christian experience, is in charge of the Church, as the most vital but the subordinate part of its living organism'. And let those who think this is ecclesiological docetism, a flight into an invisible Church, turn to the Third Book of Richard Hooker's *Ecclesiastical Polity*, where he too stresses that the Church is above all a society—'Not an assembly, but a society'.[4] The Church consists primarily of persons, and it is more important to remember this than to think of it as an institution or in terms of ontological metaphysics. It is not the whole truth about the Church; it is perhaps a doctrine of the centre, rather than the circumference. At a time when all the stress seems to be on objectivity, the

---

[3] *The Apostolic Ministry* (1909).   [4] Op. cit. 3.14.

35

emphasis on inwardness and fellowship in experience deserves consideration as something more than old-fashioned. In the first place, because it thinks of unity rather as a ray of light than as a box, it un-churches fewer Christians than the doctrines of Rome, Constantinople, Canterbury or Geneva. It answers the convictions of Christian men in contact with their separated brethren that there is a unity deeper and wider than they can define. It stands for that unity which exists now, amid all division and separation, without which none of us could Christianly exist for a moment, to which scriptures, creeds, experience, worship, behaviour can only point, since it is a unity hid with Christ in God. And it is dynamic, for it must be incomplete until all nations and races, and indeed all things in heaven and earth, are reconciled in him.[5] In short, this is the Catholicity which finds superb expression in the words of St Augustine—'Christ is the fullness of the Church, that is the Head and the Body, according to the fullness of a perfect man, in which man we are severally members'.[6]

Can we come closer to defining this unity? Is there an ecumenical, a catholic norm?

There is a game I once invented called 'Ecumenical Beggar my Neighbour'. It consists of

[5] The Reformers Lidgett would have found most congenial in this matter are Oecolampadius of Basel, who in a great field-day of Protestant preaching in Berne in 1528 chose as his theme, 'Of the love of Christ for his Church', and Martin Bucer of Strasbourg, who like Lidgett himself was most at home in the Epistle to the Ephesians.

[6] Sermon 541, Cap. 1. Migne *P.L.*, XXXIX, 1493.

making a list of points, of theological charges, which Protestants and Catholics make against one another and which are, in essence, identical. Here are a few :

(1) Protestants claim that Catholics have fallen away from biblical religion, e.g. in the Hellenizing of the gospel in the second century.

 Catholics claim that Protestants have fallen away from the Christian faith in the sixteenth century. (Both agree that there is a fall, and that it is the other who has fallen.)

(2) Protestants claim that the Catholic view of salvation fails to establish the good life, by its double standard of morality and a general ethical laxity.

 Catholics claim that Protestant theology leads to antinomianism and that the doctrine of justification by faith ignores the need for sanctification.

(3) Protestants charge Catholics with rigorism, with a false asceticism, e.g. in regard to marriage, which denies the good gifts of God.

 Catholics charge Protestants with a rigid Puritanism which denies the good gifts of God.

(4) Protestants charge Catholics with a view of salvation which is man-centred.

Catholics   charge Protestants with an emphasis on service rather than on the vision of God, which is man-centred, and with a subjectivism which is ego-centric.

(5) Protestants charge Catholics with secularizing the Gospel by entangling it with law and politics and power.

Catholics   charge Protestants with secularizing the Gospel by capitulating to human greed at the time of the Reformation, and in modern times by failing to withstand the secular state.

(6) Protestants claim that the Catholic view of grace is impersonal, legalistic, mechanical.

Catholics   claim that the Protestant doctrine of forensic justification is legalistic and external, and that its doctrine of grace takes no account of inherent righteousness.

(7) Protestants charge Catholics with denying the Real Presence of Christ in His Church as prophet, priest and king, and needing a Pope or a hierarchy to act for Him.

Catholics   claim that Protestant eucharistic doctrine implies a Real Absence of Christ from His Church and Sacraments, and that they fail to understand the meaning of Christ's humanity in reference to the doctrine of the Church.

(8) Protestants claim that Catholics take religion away from the common man by cutting off the clergy from the laity and by opposing vernacular liturgies and scriptures.

Catholics claim that Protestants take religion from the common man by setting up media of worship which demand a certain cultural level and an intellectual equipment and moral earnestness which ordinary men cannot attain.

(9) Protestants claim that Catholics have imported into the Christian religion new-fangled doctrines and practices unknown to the Primitive Church.

Catholics claim that in the sixteenth century Protestants imported new-fangled doctrines and practices unknown to the Primitive Church.

An interesting fact emerges : behind these charges and counter-claims there is the outline of a norm, of fundamental agreements, as e.g. that the Christian religion must be God-centred, that Christ is really present with His people, that grace must be personal, that salvation involves both forgiveness and holiness. It suggests moreover that this norm is not to be

sought for in a *via media*, a balance of opposing
doctrines, or in synthesis or tension between
opposites.[7] The danger of seeking such a *via media*
was pointed out by Newman: 'The *via media* has
never existed except on paper, it has never been
reduced to practice: it is known, not positively but
negatively in its differences from the rival creeds,
not in its own properties . . . what is this but to fancy
a road over mountains and rivers which has never
been cut?'[8] No, the lesson for us is surely in the
profound statement of the Evangelical Charles
Symeon that 'Truth is not in the middle, and not in
one extreme, but in both extremes'.

And this, it seems to me, is the answer to the question put by the Archbishop of Canterbury, over
twelve years ago now, to three groups of Churchmen, 'whether a synthesis is possible between
Protestantism and Catholicism'. The first reply,
entitled *Catholicity*, by a team of Anglo-Catholic
divines, was of the three answers the most profound
and provocative; the second, *The Catholicity of
Protestantism*, by a Group of Free Churchmen, was
the most scholarly; the third, *The Fulness of Christ*,

[7] This seems to me to be the weakness of the valuable study of Dr F. W.
Kantzenbach—*The Struggle about the Unity of the Church in the Century of the
Reformation* (*Das Ringen um die Einheit der Kirche in JHDT der Reformation*
[1957]). He concentrates on the moderate men, who might be called 'ecuman-
iacs before the Ecumenical movement', on Erasmus, Bucer, Melanchthon, and so
his argument finds a climax in the pathetic dilettantism of Georg Witzel, with
his elaborate definitions of the appeal to Antiquity (the Alexander Knox of the
sixteenth century); whereas the really profound examination of the nature of the
Church is to be found in Luther, Zwingli, Calvin and the Anabaptists often at
their most polemical, as in the writings of Wyclif and Huss before them.
[8] *Lectures on the Prophetical Office of the Church* (1837), p. 20.

by Anglican Evangelicals, was the most positive, but was perhaps rather dull. Dr Eric Mascall, in a recent impressive volume, *The Recovery of Unity*, has taken up the threads of that discussion. He is good enough to quote me as saying in 1948 that the manual *Catholicity* had raised questions which might bring about an argument of classic importance; but for the abortive lapse of this great argument Dr Mascall seems to blame the Free Church contribution, which he says amounted to little more than 'a vigorous defence of Luther and Calvin'. To this, however, the answer might be made: 'Ye have compelled us.' The criticisms of the Reformers in *Catholicity* were so extreme and, if true, so damaging, that they could only be met by careful examination at the level of technical scholarship. This the Free Church Group attempted, and since I contributed only a name to the title page, I may say that I think they did rather well, with the result that, far more than the other two booklets, their work has been in constant use since as a manual of reference. Unfortunately, Dr Mascall now goes out of his way to add to the number of these misconceptions about the Reformers. *Catholicity* had suggested that the Reformers shared the one-sided doctrinal stresses of the late medieval Latin Church. Dr Mascall develops this thought with an assertion borrowed from Fr Louis Bouyer,[9] to the effect that Luther and the other Reformers were inextricably involved in

9 *The Spirit and Form of Protestantism* (London, 1956), pp. 16off.

the mental framework of the late medieval philosophy of 'Nominalism', a radical empiricism which
rejected ontology and the philosophy of substance.
This is given as the explanation of Luther's disastrous
doctrine of justification by faith : it is also set forward
as an explanation of the errors of Zwingli and Erasmus. The conclusion drawn is practical and drastic.
We had better forget the Reformers, bypass their
doctrines and look elsewhere for the clues toward
the recovery of unity.[10]

To this the following brief comments may be
made. First, even if it were true that Luther was as
involved in the mental framework in which he was
trained as was St Paul in the traditions of Rabbinic
Judaism, if St Paul could powerfully think through
his gospel in terms of the dimension of Christian
experience, why should it be thought impossible for
Martin Luther? Second, Nominalism was only one
of important late medieval traditions : a better case
could be made out for the influence of the 'modern
devotion' on Erasmus, humanism on Zwingli, and
the study of Augustine on Luther. Third, Dr Mascall's description of Nominalism[11] is not abreast of
Roman Catholic scholarship—above all, the studies
of Paul Vignaux of the Sorbonne, and the Francis-
can, Philotheus Böhner of New York. In Germany

[10] *The Recovery of Unity*, pp. 25ff.

[11] It is taken apparently quite uncritically from Fr Louis Bouyer, *The Spirit
and Form of Protestantism*, pp. 160ff, paragraphs which contain major howlers and
which caricature the late medieval schoolmen. The only excuse for this kind of
thing is to say with the late Philip Guedalla: 'Any stigma will do to beat a
dogma.'

Joseph Lortz and Erwin Iserloh in an important study, published in 1956, of *Grace and Eucharist . . . in William of Ockham*, criticize Ockham in two great points. He plays down the gravity of sin and whittles away its influence on fallen man, and his preoccupation with a dialectic of divine power pays too little attention to Christology. Could there be anything more opposite to Luther? Fourth, Luther's theological revolt began with his lectures of 1509, a vehement protest against the intrusion of this very philosophy into the field of biblical truth. Fifth, what kind of a philosophy is this which could provide the opposite sacramental views of Martin Luther and Ulrich Zwingli? Can Dr Mascall bring forward the slightest evidence of Nominalist influence on the Swiss Reformer; and if he can, will he explain how similar sacramental views arose in the case of his allies, Andrew Carlstadt who was a Scotist, and Martin Bucer, trained in the study of St Thomas Aquinas?

This serious criticism apart, it is important to return to the main argument of *Catholicity*, in its concern for the 'wholeness' of the original Church, a wholeness not only of doctrine, but of worship, experience and life. We should listen carefully to Dr Mascall when he tells us that this 'wholeness' was not something belonging only to the early Church, but persisted through later centuries, 'through all distortions and partial expressions'. We must take seriously his affirmation that the method of returning to this 'wholeness', to the recovery of the ecumenical norm involves 'diligently working back through the history of the Church, and using at every stage whatever powers of discrimination we possess, in order to extricate the authentic norm so far as we are able, and to see how it can be best expressed in the theology of our own day, and embodied in the life of the modern Church'[12]—for here Dr Mascall has not only sketched a valuable ecumenical programme. He has also unawares described the Protestant Reformation![13] For just so did the Reformers seek to return to the catholicity of the primitive Church. Theirs was a coherent pattern of doctrine, worship, experience, and life. They too believed that it was a pattern which persisted through the centuries, even amid the errors and corruptions of the medieval Church. Returning to the Bible, they also used what powers of discrimination they had, the new tools provided by the humanists, the sacred languages, and the new printed editions of the 'old Fathers', and they too restated the Christian faith in the biblical theology of their time, and sought to relate it to their contemporary world.

This is no debating point, for it is the coherence of the Protestant tradition which is in question between us. The dialogue between Catholics and Protestants can never be really fruitful until Catholics reckon, not with the salvation of individual Protestants, or

[12] *The Recovery of Unity*, p. 42.   [13] And also the Wesleys!

the persistence in Protestantism of isolated Catholic truths, but with the Protestant Churches as societies, and with the coherence of its tradition as a whole.[14]

If this coherence of Protestantism is not as easily apparent as the unity of a regimented Catholicism, it is partly because through the events of the Reformation there was a new birth of freedom. Polemic has made the most of the variations of Protestantism, but this very freedom to divide and differ involves a Christian toleration which, though in the first place provoked by historical events rather than by a Christian conviction about toleration, was to find a superb rationale in Milton's 'Areopagitica' : 'There be who perpetually complain of sects and schisms and make it such a calamity that any man dissents from their maxims ... they are the troublers, they are the dividers of unity. . . . To be still searching what we know not by what we know, still closing up truth to truth as we find it, this is the golden rule ... not the forced and outward unity of cold and neutral and inwardly divided minds.'

Variations of Protestantism, different evangelical patterns, existed almost from the start. Within months of Luther's protest other programmes of Reform had emerged, in the cities of South Germany and Switzerland, in the radical groups which were to focus in the Anabaptists, and later on yet other forms

---

[14] This is the limitation of modern Roman Catholic scholars said to be ecumenically minded. They are bound to believe the Reformers heretical and therefore to seek for explanations of the heresy in such far-fetched and unscholarly hypotheses as that of Fr Bouyer mentioned above.

were fashioned as the Reformation took its own shape in England, France, and Scandinavia, and when in due time it passed to the New World. Yet there was a deep, underlying coherence. 'As for those persons', wrote John Jewell, 'whom they upon spite call Zwinglians and Lutherans, . . . they vary not betwixt themselves upon the principles and foundations of our religion, nor as touching God, nor Christ, nor the Holy Ghost, nor in the article of justification, nor of everlasting life.'[15]

There was the common acceptance of the Holy Scriptures, the common reliance on the great confessions of the Early Church.[16] Despite all the aberrations of the radicals, it is remarkable to what extent men like Thomas Müntzer and Hans Huth and Pilgram Marbeck lived out of this common core of Christian faith.

But the coherence was more than one of doctrine. Doctrine, experience, worship, obedience, balanced and to some extent supplemented one another in a new framework of Christian edification. A movement which in its first generation could produce such marvels as Tyndale's New Testament, Luther's Bible and Children's Catechism, the Strasbourg Hymn-book, and the Book of Common Prayer, is not liturgically to be despised. It is true that sometimes the results were partial and one-sided. The major

[15] *Apology for the Church of England*, Part 3 (P.S.) p. 69.
[16] J. Koopmans in his study of *The Dogma of the Early Church in the Reformation* (*Das Altkirchliche Dogma in der Reformation* [1955]) has shown how fundamental for the great Reformers were Nicea and Chalcedon.

operation on the Canon of the ancient liturgies, made needful by medieval error and abuse, had liturgical results which take too little account of the present heavenly Priesthood of our Lord. Yet the preaching of Justification by only Faith was in itself the pleading of the present efficacy of the Cross. The first painting of Protestantism in action, Cranach's altar piece in Wittenberg, shows Luther preaching, pointing away from himself to the figure of the crucified. Protestant preaching is nothing less than, in John Wesley's tremendous definition, 'to offer Christ . . . to set forth Christ as evidently crucified before men's eyes'. Luther's doctrine of Justification is expressed in a series of magnificent intuitions, profound and not yet fully explored. It is for him so rich and many sided a conception that it tends to draw all else within itself, including the later category of Sanctification, since for him it is not a mere preliminary to the Christian life, but the whole standing ground of the Christian's experience of the indwelling Church, a pardoned, and pardoning relationship in which the Holy Spirit brings ever new creative energies within the regenerated soul. Later Protestant orthodoxies might draw out and systematize this doctrine ; later still, they had to erect checks and safeguards for it, because, since it is the optic nerve of the gospel of grace, it has from the time of St Paul been vulnerable to misunderstanding and abuse. But this, too, must be set against the background of new institutions of Christian discipline,

47

instruction and edification, which in four centuries have nourished millions of men and women, and great societies, with results of which we have no reason at all to be apologetic or still less ashamed.

This is not to ignore the sins of Protestantism which have been very many and very grievous. It is not to forget that there was much that was partial and one-sided and negative in its return to primitive catholicity. In fact there is an element of Pre-Raphaelitism in all backward movements. The return to Primitive Christianity has meant very different things in Christian history, to the great Reformers and the Anabaptists, to the Puritans and to the Non-Jurors, to the Moravians and to John Wesley, to Maria Theresa's minister, Kaunitz, to Mirabeau and the French National Assembly, and to the Oxford Movement. All, in one sense, re-discovered a primitive Church which never was. And yet none entirely failed. All found enough of truth to afford a cutting edge against contemporary abuse, and a practical programme of reform.

Between the authors of the manual *Catholicity* and those belonging to the Protestant tradition, there is more in common, then, than its authors might suppose. When we are aware of this, we can go on to consider together the great questions : What are the safeguards of the holy tradition ? How does the Church detect poison in the blood stream ? And here from the Protestant side are some things to be said.

There is in the first place the Gospel of grace. It is no accident that the Reformation began with Martin Luther, with the problem of a 'bruised conscience', with the forgiveness of sins, with the righteousness of God. The true Church brings peace to the conscience, new life which springs from wondering gratitude, life in the Holy Spirit, freedom from bondage to fear and superstition and from the traditions of men. A Protestantism which ceased to do these things would also be in judgement.

Inseparably linked with the Gospel are the Holy Scriptures. It was a brilliant device of Newman to turn the argument of a thousand years of appeal '*ad fontes*' to the fountain heads, with the affirmation that, 'It is indeed sometimes said that the stream is clearest near the spring, . . . it does not apply to the history of a philosophy or belief which on the contrary is more equable and purer and stronger when its bed has become deep and broad and full.'[17] But the answer had been given already in the most forthright of all Reformation creeds, the Scots Confession. 'For the Reformation of any abuse in the Kirk we ought not sa meikle to luke what men before us have said and done as unto what the Holy Ghost speaks within the body of the Scriptures and unto what Christ Jesus himself did and commanded to be done.' Dare anybody claim that later tradition can ever be 'purer and stronger' than it was in the work of Jesus Christ Himself, a well of truth

[17] *The Development of Doctrine* (1887), p. 40.

undefiled, to whom the Scriptures bear witness, themselves a stream perpetually renewed in the Church, through the Holy Spirit?

But the Scriptures alone are insufficient to protect the Church from error. 'The Presbyterians', said Alexander Knox, 'became Arians with the Bible in their hands.'[18] Richard Baxter, in *The Life of Faith*, stresses the importance of Church history: 'Suspect not all church history or tradition in an extreme opposition of the Papists . . . our "*traditio tradens*" is primarily nothing but a certain history or usage of the universal Christian Church . . . and therefore it is to be lamented exceedingly that any orthodox teachers should tell us that . . . these are not sufficient . . . without the testimony of the Spirit: as if all this were none of the testimony of the Spirit.'[19]

There is, further, the appeal to history itself. The Incarnation means that God Himself 'born of a woman, born under the law', accepts the limitations of the historic process. The stream of Church existence flows within the river of history, and is influenced by other currents than its own. As the human body draws life and nourishment from its material environment, so the Church draws on the energies of its surrounding cultures, and is affected by their rise and fall. And it can draw in germs, infections, viruses too. That is why the appeal to history must be free and unfettered, in complete

[18] *Remains of Alexander Knox*, I.432.
[19] *Practical Works*, Vol. XII (1830 edn), p. 97.

loyalty to truth and to its findings. Where this is absent the way is open to mythologizing, to the canonizing of the Church's own subjective experience, to such delusions that by pondering the implications of revelation it can become aware of new and alleged historical facts, such as the perpetual virginity of our Lady, and her bodily assumption.[20]

The characteristically Anglican contribution to the Protestant tradition is not so much the appeal to history, which it shares with the Continental Reformers, but the appeal to reason, in that impressive tradition which begins with Richard Hooker, and continues through Chillingworth and the Falkland circle to the Cambridge Platonists and Bishop Butler. I cannot say how since Kant and Hegel the appeal to reason has been undermined by the criticisms of existentialism, deep psychology or logical positivism, but at least the appeal to reason means this, that the Church cannot adopt less austere measurements of integrity than those of the historian, the scientist, or the philosopher within their own disciplines; that it can never capitulate to emotionalism, fanaticism, or obscurantist pietism.

What of new truth? Protestantism is more sensitive to the spirit of each age, easily succumbs to pressures of history, against which Rome has grown an extra skin. But it is also more open to new truths emerging in history itself. And one must ask whether canons of 'catholic tradition' derived from

20 See W. von Loewenich, *Modern Catholicism* (1959), Chs. 4 and 7.

the patristic age are not derived from a thought world on the one hand too insulated and introverted, and on the other hand more influenced by secular influences than orthodoxy can easily admit; one would press these questions in relation to the ministry, to the place of women and of the laity in the Church, and of the modern concepts of democracy. It is one thing to say that the Church ought not to accommodate its faith to the spirit of the age, must not come to terms with secular thought on the world's terms; it is another to behave as though the Church had nothing to learn, nothing to re-think, nothing to discard after its encounters with great movements of the human spirit. Surely a sensitiveness toward such possibilities is a mark of catholicity. 'An exclusive spirit toward men,' said Lidgett, 'whether of other Churches or no Church, whether Christian or non-Christian races, will shut us out from knowing in all its fullness the grace of Christ.'[21]

We advance, then, along the way of dialogue. First, a dialogue within the Ecumenical Movement. How sad it would be if the Free Churches were to pursue mainly denominational interests, seeking to bolster the minority Churches of Europe by reminding the World Council that their Big Brothers are watching them, without any real interest in coming close to the great Lutheran and Reformed Churches, and beyond to Orthodoxy and Rome, the mother Church of the West.

[21] *Catholicity: The Mark of Spirituality* (1907).

Then a dialogue with our fellow Protestants. The phrase 'Pan-Protestant' is always used disparagingly, and I do not much care for it, but let us remember that a united non-Roman Church would be the most adventurous Christian experiment yet, since it would involve elements of consent and liberty, diversities of worship and behaviour, such as no Church has ever yet contained. (It would be the most comprehensive Church since Noah's Ark!)

Then a dialogue with the Church of England. It is a pity that the apportionment of the three booklets written for the Archbishop disguised the most important of all tensions in English religion, the antiphon often tragic but always fruitful between the Establishment and historic Dissent. Now that this tension has lessened, now that the Free Churches are no longer an effective 'Her Majesty's Opposition', and the Church of England has become another denomination alongside us in a mainly secularized society, we must ask whether this historic tension might not be revivified in unity, and we must take seriously the noble vision of the Lambeth Conference of one Church, 'truly evangelical and truly catholic' within these islands.

And then a dialogue among ourselves. I strongly support the plea of Dr Ernest Payne for theological discussions between the Free Churches. We need to take stock of our common heritage, Puritan, Evangelical, Nonconformist, in the light of biblical theology. A few years ago an article in the

Architectural Review gave the world the grim new word 'Subtopia'. It showed the drab uniformity of our urban civilization, the roads and road signs, the petrol pumps and concrete lamp standards, the town centres almost identical in any suburb of San Francisco, New York, Johannesburg, London, Berlin, Tokyo. Are we not creating a kind of religious subtopia—a suburban moralistic mediocrity of thought and experience and behaviour, a pattern of Nonconformity which varies very little from Atlanta, Georgia, to Port Elizabeth and Salisbury and London, which fails in a crisis to produce heroic witness, as it seems to be failing in the matter of race relations in South Africa and the Rhodesias, not at the level of official pronouncements, but in the quality of the average Church member? What has happened to that discipline which was once our glory? It is a great thing to have escaped from pietism, but in these days of the human parson and the too too human congregation, might we not turn uneasily to John Wesley's sermons of 'Friendship with the World', and 'Separation from the World'? 'Look around,' he said, 'and see the melancholy effects on your brethren : how are the mighty fallen : they would take no warning : they would converse intimately with earthly minded men, till they measured their steps to earth again.' 'God has given us length and breadth,' said Scott Lidgett once ; 'may he give us depth and height.'

And so we turn to the last dialogue : with the

Lord of the Church—a dialogue of penitence and faith. Here is no question of claims and counter claims, of argument. Here we stand in the solidarity of the one Israel of God before Him who received double for all our sins. Cardinal Newman once suggested that the penalty which the Old Israel suffered for the sin of disunity was the suspension of grace. It may be that the grace of revival and of renewal will not be given to us in our separation, will not be given until we stand together for the mending of the Church and for the healing of the nations. However that may be, our present and our future unity is in Him. It is part of the deep mystery of His being that Church history, the whole of Church history, divided in our experience, is one in Him.

He was in the beginning when the morning stars sang together, and all the sons of God shouted for joy ; He was with Abraham who rejoiced to see His day, with Isaac and Jacob dwelling in tents ; He journeyed with His pilgrim people in the wilderness, as a Rock which followed them, and as a pillar of cloud and of fire ; He spake by the prophets. He was made flesh, suffered, died, and rose again. He was the first Christian, the first Catholic, the first Protestant, the only one who has shared in every part each detail of our separated stories, and who bestrides the future in that wider unity in which, because it is in Him, we shall be at home. For what His people do in memory of Him is a lesser thing than that which He for ever does in His memorial of us—who keeps us in His mind, and bears us on His heart, and offers us together with Himself to the glory of the Eternal Father in the unity of His Body, the fullness of Him who all in all is being fulfilled.